D0883649

EDGE
BOOKS

SPORTS TO THE EXTREME

EXTREME
Snow AND Ice
Sports

BY ERIN K. BUTLER

CAPSTONE PRESS
a capstone imprint

Edge Books are published by Capstone Press,
1710 Roe Crest Drive, North Mankato, Minnesota 56003
www.mycapstone.com

Library of Congress Cataloging-in-Publication Data
Library of Congress Cataloging-in-Publication data is available on the Library of Congress website.
ISBN 978-1-51577-859-2 (library binding)
ISBN 978-1-51577-863-9 (eBook PDF)

Editorial Credits
Nikki Ramsay, editor; Sara Radka, designer; Laura Manthe, production specialist

Photo Credits
Getty Images: Christopher Bernard, 9, Cultura RF, 13, Westend61, 25, iStockphoto, cover, 1, Jan Hetfleisch/
Bongarts, 21, Joerg Mitter/Red Bull, 26, Sebastian Marko/Red Bull, 27; Newscom: Hiroyuki Sato/AFLO, 6,
ZUMAPRESS/Greg Smith, 15, ZUMAPRESS/Joel Marklund/Bildbyran, 19, Dave Phillips/MCT, 22; Shutterstock:
Alessandro Colle, 5, divedog, 28, Dmytro Vietrov, 6, IM_photo, 11, Mark Bonham, 17, Tyler Meade Photography,
18, YanLev, 7

Design elements by Book Buddy Media.

Printed in the United States of America.
010364F17

Table of Contents

Extreme Snow & Ice Sports

When the weather turns cold and the earth is covered with ice and snow, most people like to stay inside. These can be **treacherous** conditions. But there is one group of people that love this environment — extreme winter athletes.

Extreme snow and ice sports are physically demanding activities. They involve high speed and high risk, and are performed on snow or icy **terrain**. These sports depend on natural landscapes and the weather to create the perfect extreme environment. With slippery surfaces, snow-covered hills, and piercing cold, slick snow and ice sports are in a class of their own.

Most extreme winter sports require special equipment. Some are performed on boards. Some use carefully designed machinery. And others require tools specifically for ice. No matter the tools or equipment involved, snow and ice sports are some of the world's most extreme activities.

treacherous—marked by danger and difficulty in approaching

terrain—the surface of the land

Ice climbers need to know as much as they can about the terrain before they start climbing.

5

Extreme snowboarders can ride either on a half-pipe or in the natural environment.

EXTREME(LY) YOUNG

Some of the world's best extreme athletes participate in a competition called the X Games. The X Games are held in both the summer and the winter.

In 2014 American snowboarder Chloe Kim won a silver medal at the X Games. She was the youngest athlete to ever medal at the extreme competition. Since then, she has become the only athlete to win three gold medals at the X Games before the age of 16.

CHAPTER 1

Extreme Snowboarding

Snowboarders slide down snowy slopes at high speeds while strapped to a board. Invented in the 1960s, snowboarding mixed parts of skateboarding and surfing to glide across the snow. The idea quickly became popular. People began snowboarding all over the world.

Snowboards vary in size to change their stability and maneuverability.

Some people snowboard for fun or as a hobby. But others take this sport to the extreme. They aim for high speeds. They perform tricks, stunts, and impressive maneuvers. The hills on which they snowboard usually have more difficult terrain. There may also be obstacles for snowboarders to navigate, such as cliffs and ravines.

A snowboard is similar to a skateboard, but it has no wheels. Snowboards are also longer. A snowboard is, on average, 5 feet (1.5 meters) long, while a skateboard is smaller at about 2.5 feet (0.76 m) long.

Snowboards can be made of wood, plastic, or foam. Different designs do different things. In speed-snowboarding and racing, the board is stiff and has hard boots that strap to the board and offer support. Freestyle boards have soft boots that strap to the board and are made of more flexible materials.

Extreme snowboarders enter competitions to showcase their creativity and skill. The three main categories of competition are alpine, freestyle, and boardercross.

Alpine competitions are based on speed and skill. Snowboarders fly downhill as fast as possible while weaving between **gates**. Freestyle competitions are more creative, with snowboarders using a half-pipe to perform daring tricks. Judges score each routine to select the winner. In boardercross, four to six snowboarders race down a hill while performing jumps and navigating obstacles.

Alpine snowboarders use longer boards for greater speeds. Freestyle boards are shorter, making tricks easier to perform. Boardercross boards are somewhere in between.

Not all extreme snowboarders compete. Some simply enjoy reaching high speeds on their boards, or creating new tricks. Many share pictures or videos of their snowboarding online.

Some snowboarders like seeking out new trails with fresh snow. They often find untouched snow in **backcountry** areas off the main trails. If they are not careful, they run the risk of starting an avalanche by boarding.

gates—narrow poles with a flag attached

backcountry—an isolated area often at high altitude that is not marked by trails or patrolled by park rangers or other authorities

Snowboarders must be ready for wintry weather. They wear lots of layers, gloves, and goggles for warmth.

SNOWBOARDING IN THE OLYMPICS

Many extreme sports are not included in the Olympics, but that is slowly changing. Snowboarding entered the Winter Olympics for the first time in 1998 in Nagano, Japan. The first Olympic snowboarders — both men and women — competed in giant **slalom** and half-pipe events. Boardercross and similar competitions were added to the Winter Games in 2010 and 2014.

slalom—a downhill race in which riders weave through sets of poles

CHAPTER 2

Extreme Skiing

When you think about skiing, you might think of vacations or resorts. But this winter sport can get much more extreme than just gentle hills. At a ski resort, the most difficult hills might have slopes of around 30 to 40 degrees. In extreme skiing, skiers speed down slopes at an angle of at least 45 degrees — if not more. To make things more difficult, the slopes are usually not part of known paths. The snow is ungroomed, and there may be patches of ice or rock underneath.

The sport developed because people wanted a bigger thrill. Over the years, it has changed to become even more exciting. With the right skis, skiers can reach speeds of more than 60 miles (97 kilometers) per hour. They also perform tricks and stunts.

It can be difficult to reach the slopes that are needed for extreme skiing. A chairlift might not be enough to get you to the top. Sometimes, the only way to get there is by helicopter.

Getting from place to place is not the only challenge in extreme skiing. There's a lot of risk involved too. Taking paths no one has been on before can lead to unpredictable results. Skiers have to make lightning-quick decisions to avoid obstacles. And there is always the risk of causing an avalanche. Probes are carried to skiers so they can test snow conditions. Every skier carries a shovel to dig himself or herself out of an avalanche.

When skiers perform jumps at high speeds, they take the sport to its most extreme.

Athletes usually do not ski alone. They need to be able to call for help in an emergency. If a skier does ski alone, a GPS device is a necessary piece of equipment. This helps emergency responders find them in case they are buried in snow.

CHAPTER 3

Snowkiting

In the summer, many people love to go kitesurfing on the water. Athletes travel across the waves on a board while being pulled by a large kite. Extreme winter athletes liked the idea of kitesurfing, but they did not have access to bodies of water. Instead, they **adapted** the sport for snow. Snowkiting was born.

Advanced snowkiters aim for high speeds and big jumps. Regular snowkiters can reach speeds of 30 miles (48 km) per hour. However, advanced snowkiters can reach up to 70 miles (113 km) per hour. Deeper snow and larger kites add to the challenge.

There are different styles and sizes of kites that a snowkiter can choose from. In general, kites used for snowkiting are smaller than those for kitesurfing. This is because ice and snow have much less **friction** than water. It takes less energy to get a snowkiter moving.

Skis offer the snowkiter more control, while snowboards give an experience more like kitesurfing. The last and most essential piece of equipment for every snowkiter is a helmet, which protects them in case of a fall.

adapt—to change to fit into a new or different environment

friction—a force produced when two objects rub against each other; friction slows down objects

Most kites are soft and do not have hard frames.

13

CHAPTER 4

Snow Kayaking

Extreme kayaking is a well-known summer sport. But what do boaters do in the winter? They take their boats to the slopes! Instead of traveling down a river, snow kayakers use a waxed boat to speed down steep, snowy slopes.

Sliding down the slopes in a snow kayak can feel like sledding. It comes with high risks and an adrenaline rush. Snow kayakers can reach speeds of up to 50 miles (80 km) per hour. Kayaks can be difficult to control at these high speeds. Even with paddles, which give them more control than just a regular sled, steering can be hard.

Most snow kayakers go kayaking in the backcountry. In these areas, paths have not been set up. But there are also special areas that have been set aside specifically for snow kayak racing.

AVALANCHE!

Many athletes who participate in extreme snow sports run the risk of getting caught in an avalanche. An avalanche is a sudden, potentially deadly flow of snow. The worst avalanches can travel as fast as 186 miles (300 km) per hour. Extreme winter athletes are especially at risk of starting an avalanche because they are disturbing new, heavy snow.

In Colorado's Kayaks on Snow competition, athletes kayak down snow-covered slopes and then into icy water to finish the race.

CHAPTER 5

Extreme Snowmobiling

Snowmobiles are powerful vehicles. These huge machines often weigh around 450 pounds (200 kilograms). They are built to travel on rough, snowy terrain. A standard snowmobile has an engine, rubber tracks in the back, skis in the front, a seat, and handlebars.

Originally, snowmobiles were used for transportation or fun. Then, people began to realize that they could be used for a lot more. They started blazing their own trails in the backcountry. Jumps were built and tricks were performed. Motocross — but on snow — was born.

The two main types of extreme snowmobiling are freestyle and snocross. In freestyle, riders launch off ramps and get huge air of 100 feet (30.5 m) or more. They perform tricks while in the air, such as frontflips and backflips, and flashy landings.

Snocross riders try to reach the fastest speeds possible as they race against each other. Tracks include jumps, tight turns, and obstacles. Riders have reached speeds of more than 100 miles (160 km) per hour.

EXTREME FACT!

In 1968 Ralph Plaisted and a group of adventurers became the first people to make it to the North Pole on snowmobiles.

An essential part of a good snowmobile jump is the landing. The goal is to make it as smooth as possible.

Backcountry riding is a third type of extreme exploration. It is generally done for fun, not for competition. Snowmobilers ride in areas where no one has gone before. They love finding new places to ride. They are true trailblazers. But riders have to be very careful. Just like other backcountry winter sports, there is a risk of avalanches.

Backcountry riders carry backpacks full of survival gear. Radios, emergency food, first-aid kits, whistles, tarps, and satellite phones are only a few items on the must-have list.

TOP X GAMES SNOWMOBILING MOMENTS

Snocross is the oldest motorized X Games sport. Men and women compete separately in both snocross and freestyle events. They earn medals for racing and performing stunts. The X Games offer an opportunity for extreme snowmobilers to gather with other extreme winter athletes. They can show off their skills and learn from some of the best athletes in their sport.

Over the years, snowmobilers have made their mark in the Winter X Games. In 2000 a snocross rider named Tucker Hibbert became the youngest person to win a gold medal in the winter games. He has won nine X Games gold medals since. In 2011 brothers Caleb and Colten Moore performed a tandem backflip on a snowmobile. The next big challenge riders are tackling is a double backflip. The sky is the limit for extreme snowmobilers!

CHAPTER 6

Bobsledding

Bobsledding, also called bobsleighing, is a sport in which athletes speed down an ice-covered track. They use a vehicle called a bobsled. Bobsleds are sleek and built to go as fast as possible. They can hold two or four riders. The rider in front is called the driver, while the rider in back is the brakeman. Riders in between are called crewmen. Heavy bobsleds can reach about 100 miles (160 km) per hour.

This extreme sport is an old one. It dates back to the 1880s. People began organizing and competing quickly. The first bobsled competition was held in 1898 in Saint Moritz, Switzerland. Bobsledding was one of the first extreme Olympic sports. It was added in 1924.

It might not seem like bobsledding requires much athleticism. But in reality, it is an incredibly difficult sport. It can also be dangerous, since bobsleds are so heavy — up to 1,389 pounds (630 kg). Athletes must be very strong to get the bobsled going from a stationary position. They run in spiked shoes to give the sled the best possible start. Then they must pull themselves into the moving sled. Riders work together to shift their weight and steer. Fractions of a second can mean the difference between winning and losing a race. Usually, bobsledders are ranked based on their total time racing in four heats.

Bobsledding courses are often around 4,920 feet (1,500 m) long, and include about 15 turns.

The longest running ski bike festival takes place in Durango, Colorado, at Purgatory Resort. For more than 15 years, ski bikers have enjoyed a weekend of racing and community.

CHAPTER 7

Ski Biking

Most people would never expect to see someone bike through the snow. But, in the creative style of extreme sports, athletes have found a way. In ski biking, a rider sits on a bicycle-like frame. Instead of wheels, the bike has skis — one ski in the front and one in the back. The rider uses this unpowered vehicle to travel down the same slopes where other people ski.

Of all the extreme ice and snow sports, ski biking is one of the safest. The design of a ski bike makes it very stable. The first models were wooden and heavy. Over time, they have been improved to become much lighter. Many people use mountain bike and BMX bike frames. The handlebars control the front ski. The back ski is controlled by the rider shifting his or her weight to the right or left.

Ski biking is a relatively new sport, and athletes love coming up with creative ways to make it even more extreme. Flips, spins, and jumps are just a few of the moves that extreme ski bikers are learning to perform.

EXTREME FACT!

Ski bikers can reach very high speeds when skiing downhill. The record stands at 138 miles (222 km) per hour.

CHAPTER 8

Ice Climbing

Seasoned rock climbers know the thrill of conquering a mountainside. However, not all mountainsides are dirt and rock. Some are covered in ice and snow. In cold weather, extreme climbers move up ice-covered rocks, glaciers, and frozen waterfalls.

Ice climbing requires physical strength and special equipment. Climbers take their ice tools very seriously. These tools — ice axes, crampons, and ice screws — can mean the difference between life and death. Ice axes have a pick on one side and an **adze** on the other. Crampons are spikes attached to the climber's shoes. They allow a climber to get **traction** on the ice. Ice screws help climbers in case of a fall. They are drilled into the ice and a rope is clipped to them. The rope attaches to the climber's harness.

Climbers develop different techniques depending on the angle of the ice. For example, flat footing is good for low angles, while front pointing works well for steep angles. The best ice climbers aim for fast speeds on tall, steep climbs. In 2015 Dani Arnold set a world speed record by climbing a 3,609-foot (1,100-meter) wall of ice in 1 hour and 46 minutes.

adze—the flat, curved blade on an ice axe; climbers use the adze to chop ice and cut steps

traction— the amount of grip one surface has while moving over another surface

Scotland's Aonach Mor has cliffs that reach 1,640 feet (500 m) high. Its remote location and variety of terrain make it an inviting challenge.

CHAPTER 9

Crashed Ice

Ice skaters have gone extreme too. Crashed ice sets skaters against each other as they race at high speeds. They have to navigate drops, turns, and obstacles. The first skater to the finish line wins.

In crashed ice competitions, skaters participate in races throughout the season to gain points. The skater with the most points at the end of the season is the world champion.

Crashed ice skaters can reach speeds of 50 miles (80 km) per hour. Races can become cutthroat as competitors rush for the finish.

The first crashed ice competition took place in 2001. Since then tracks have been built through cities and down mountains. Each track is filled with treacherous hurdles designed to challenge each racer. Tracks can be as long as 1,969 feet (600 meters). Only the best skaters can tackle them. Head and body protection is a must.

Every year crashed ice track designers work to make new tracks even more extreme.

Crashed ice races take place all over the world during a season.

Many of the most popular ice diving locations are in Canada and Russia.

CHAPTER 10

Ice Diving

One extreme winter sport does not involve speed, stunts, or climbing. This sport is ice diving, a specialized form of scuba diving. To begin, a diver cuts a hole in the ice, which can be between 4 and 10 feet (1.2 and 3 m) thick. This is his or her only entry or exit point to the water. Using special equipment, the diver then enters the water and explores the depths.

Ice diving requires basic scuba diving training, but there's even more to it. Ice divers need to be able to withstand the frigid waters. Temperatures fall around 0 degrees Fahrenheit (minus 18 degrees Celsius). They also must look for dangerous situations, such as unsafe ice conditions. Extreme cold can cause equipment to fail. In this dangerous environment, it is important that no equipment is left behind. A diver needs a dry suit for warmth, a knife, and gauges to track their progress. Tethers ensure divers can make their way back to their original launch site.

Although ice diving is risky, it has huge benefits not seen anywhere else. Ice diving gives divers better visibility underwater. This can lead to some breathtaking sights. Ice divers get to see underwater earth and ice formations, light displays, and rare sea life that regular scuba divers never see. Like so many extreme sports, dedicated training in ice diving leads to a great payoff.

Extreme snow and ice sports are some of the most creative and challenging in the world of extreme sports. As long as snow and ice exist, athletes will be inventing new things and taking their sports to the extreme.

Glossary

adapt (uh-DAPT)—to change to fit into a new or different environment

adze (ADZ)—the flat, curved blade on an ice axe; climbers use the adze to chop ice and cut steps

backcountry (BAK-kaunt-ree)—an isolated area often at high altitude that is not marked by trails or patrolled by park rangers or other authorities

friction (FRIK-shuhn)—a force produced when two objects rub against each other; friction slows down objects

gates (GATES)—narrow poles with a flag attached

slalom (SLA-lom)—a downhill race in which riders weave through sets of poles

terrain (tuh-RAYN)—the surface of the land

traction (TRAK-shuhn)—the amount of grip one surface has while moving over another surface

treacherous (TRECH-uhr-us)—marked by danger and difficulty in approaching

Read More

Bailer, Darice. *Snowboard Cross.* Minneapolis: Lerner Publications, 2017.

Carpenter, Jake. *Snowmobile Best Trick.* Minneapolis: Lerner Publications, 2017.

Loh-Hagan, Virginia. *Extreme Downhill Ski Racing.* North Mankato, Minn: 45th Parallel Press, 2016.

Scheff, Matt. *Torah Bright.* Extreme Sports Stars. Minneapolis: Sportszone, 2014.

Internet Sites

FactHound offers a safe, fun way to find Internet sites related to this book. All of the sites on FactHound have been researched by our staff.

Here's all you do:

Visit *www.facthound.com*

Type in this code: 9781515778592

Check out projects, games and lots more at
www.capstonekids.com

Index